The Smoke Free Habit:

21 Stop Smoking Hypnosis Strategies

To Quit Smoking and Be Smoke Free in 21 Days

Nancy Philpott, R.N.

www.SmokeFreeHabit.com

What Would You Attempt to Do If You Believed You Couldn't Fail?

Your beliefs become your thoughts.
Your thoughts become your actions.
Your actions become your habits.
Your habits become your values.
Your values become your destiny.

Table of Contents

The Smoke Free Habit:

21 Stop Smoking Hypnosis Strategies

Quit Smoking and Be Smoke Free in 21 Days

Preface

Have you ever stopped to listen to the conversations you have with yourself about quitting smoking and living life smoke free? Do you hear your inner cheerleader cheering you on telling you that you're ready to quit, and you have everything you need? Does that strategic planner inside you create a plan and set a date to stop? Does your internal emotional resilience regulator make you feel safe enough and that you're good enough to do anything you want including stopping smoking and remaining smoke free forever?

If that kind of conversation NEVER happens in your head, congratulations you are the exact reason this book was created. Those positive conversation never happened to me either.

Instead, the shame, blame, shoulda, monster kept yelling at me in an attempt to shame me into stop smoking submission. If I had that conversation with myself once I had it a thousand times.

My inner cheerleader went MIA (missing in action) along with my strategic planner and emotional resilience regulator. They took their care and compassion and hit the road without me many years ago when it came to smoking.

The truth is after 37 years as a smoker I had almost given up. I wanted desperately to quit smoking. My "Why I Need to Quit" list was HUGE compared to my "Bucket List." My I Will Quit Smoking Internal Optimist hit the road so fast, the last time I tried to quit, that I found myself gagging on nicotine and secondary smoke.

If you bought this book as a last resort and feeling completely skeptical.

Congratulations, you are the reason I wrote this book and I know exactly how and what you're feeling.

This book is about you quitting for the LAST TIME and LIVING SMOKE FREE FOREVER. Whether you tried to quit with gum, pills, patches, cold turkey, e-cigarettes or hypnosis and nothing has worked to date. The Stop Smoking Blueprint included in this book will change that for you.

If you bought this book because you are committed and ready to feel better, breathe easier, have more energy and vitality, have more confidence, have your breath and clothes smell better, live longer, and be healthier that is exactly what will happen.

Plus, you will have more confidence, more self-esteem, more trust and believe in yourself, and you feel more comfortable taking chances again.

The following pages are designed to help you take the necessary steps to do all those things and more plus save you money.

The process I've outlined in this book includes four steps and takes just 21 days to quit smoking permanently. Just like a color by number picture. It's easy if you do it. Here's how I know. I used it myself when I made a commitment to stop for good and I kept my promise to myself.

We are going to leverage what your body knows how to do and already does automatically. Create and execute habits. That's the MAIN REASON THIS IS GOING TO WORK. It's really easy.

You, with the help of your body will, execute and condition the steps in this book until it becomes your automatic default program.

Let's get started!

> *Send a copy of your receipt to join-quitsmoking@instantcustomer.com and my wonderful assistant will verify your order and send you a link to a special unadvertised bonus I made especially for you. It's my gift to Thank You and Celebrate You for having the courage to trust me, trust yourself, and finally quit smoking and live smoke free forever. Send your receipt now to join-quitsmoking@instantcustomer.com*

The Opportunity

Welcome. My name is Nancy Philpott and I want to take you on a journey that I believe WILL help you to stop smoking, create a permanent Smoke Free Habit, transform your life, health, and destiny forever.

That's a big, fat, bold claim and I WANT you to be skeptical. Having said that when you spend a few minutes with this book and the companion videos, you'll agree with me or at least experience an amazing discovery about yourself you may have never known or considered.

That discovery will begin a subtle transformation, shift your perception about your life, and allow you to begin making choices about your life and destiny that were not possible before you read this book.

If you don't know who I am or have never heard of me before, there's a short chapter and video you can watch to "meet" me and find out how I can help you be present and make conscious intentional choices about your life instead of compulsively reaching for a cigarette (or whatever you dip/smoke) and numbing out emotionally in "auto pilot" mode.

Here's the short video:

http://0s4.com/r/7HJFYD

Or scan this handy QR code:

I've spent more than 30+ years as a nurse and strategic intervention health coach helping individuals and groups improve their health. As a consulting hypnotist I've performed thousands of hypnotherapy sessions helping clients transform unwanted and unhealthy habits and patterns of behavior.

Before I had a chance to work with them, most didn't have a clue how or why their "auto pilot" programming was sabotaging their success, preventing them achieving their goals, and consciously creating the life they wanted.

In this book, I'm about to give you the # 1 secret-something that really is the "magic formula" that can help you quit smoking, remain smoke free permanently, improve your health and life when you apply some very basic principles. I used this exact formula to quit smoking after more than 37 + years and have shared these same strategies in thousands of hypnosis sessions with others just like you and me convinced they were destined to fail again, and again, and again. I quit permanently, helped them quit, and I can help you too.

Think about it like this: if I could give you a time machine where you could go back before you started smoking, with all the knowledge and wisdom you have today, and make a different decision about smoking… What decisions would you make today that you didn't make or made differently back then? How would you feel about who you are now and your ability to make a commitment and follow through with that commitment?

Who would believe you when you a made a promise, that doesn't believe you now because you've not been able to honor your commitment to stop smoking until now? Who would you ask to marry you because, as a smoker, you knew they wouldn't say "Yes" if you popped the question?" Would your life be different now if you had?

Would your relationships be different now if you'd never made a decision to smoke?

If you've been seeking and searching for years for the ANSWER and the SECRET that can literally turn your life and health around you've found it.

I discovered it when I was faced with the prospect of losing my mother to cancer and gave myself permission and the freedom to passionately and purposefully create a new ending to my story and hopefully yours too.

I want you to know you're not alone.

I'm here right now because of you and who you are.

You are my purpose and my passion.

Enjoy this book and videos.

Nancy

My Story

"I'm here for a week. We are going to eat, shop, laugh, and have fun and then I'm going home to die. I hope you're OK with that because I've already made up my mind." Three weeks later my mom was gone.

In the wee hours of the morning 48 hours before mom died, I agreed to fulfill two of her wishes. Both seemed almost impossible to accomplish after she passed. Wish # 1 was for me to stop smoking as soon as possible. Wish # 2 was for me and my sister to care for my step-dad after she passed. Both quickly became a blessing and a curse.

If I had known then what I know now, I would have understood that the moment my mom made her declaration and the moment I agreed to fulfill her deathbed wishes, life as I knew it had been transformed instantly, dramatically, and irrevocably.

For the first seven days after her proclamation my mom, my sister, and I ate, shopped, laughed, and enjoyed deep meaningful philosophical conversations about everything that mattered.

We cussed and discussed the fear of dying verses the fear of not living, the power of taking chances verses making a powerful choice, the power of unconditional love and acceptance verses loving with conditions, the power of trusting your heart and inner voice verses the consequence of living life from an inner space of fear and mistrust.

Two days after returning home mom was admitted to the hospital.

It was in those final 21 days, sitting at mom's bedside contemplating the real meaning of life and death, observing and discussing what it was like for her to transition from this life, that I uncovered and discovered so much about myself and my own survival pattern.

I began to notice and get insight into those unconscious beliefs, fears, values, life strategies, life stories, and behavioral patterns that had been modeled by mom, filed away and stored in my subconscious mind and running in the background of my life for more than 40+ years.

It became clear to me I'd been living on autopilot most of my adult life without even knowing it. The overachieving driven part of me determined to do more, be more, achieve more, earn more, and make a bigger difference in the world cared little, if at all, about doing anything except being present for mom and my family.

What I found so interesting, insightful, and simultaneously unsure of how to handle was the overwhelming fear and uncertainty I felt about who to be and how to show up in those last days and moments of mom's life. Part of me wanted to be fully present and make sure mom had everything she wanted or needed. Another part of me just wanted to run away from the pain of losing someone I dearly loved. So I handled those moments the same way I'd done for 30+ years.

When a wave of fear or uncertainty rolled over me, I'd excuse myself, make my way to the elevator, head to the parking lot, light a cigarette, and smoke. It was my default pattern then, the default pattern my mom modeled for me, and her mom modeled for her.

It was a tribal pattern deeply embedded in the fabric and culture of my family. Our way to handle everything feeling we had good or bad.

What I didn't know or understand then is the how, why, and when my autopilot survival program clicked on and hijacked my intention to be mentally, physically and emotionally present and resilient. My unconscious habit of smoking allowed me to unplug from my emotions, provided the needed distraction to avoid my fear and uncertainty, and prevented me from honoring my intentions.

I gave myself permission to keep smoking during mom's transition and avoided facing and fulfilling mom's stop smoking wish until after she passed.

There were four simple steps I used to shift out of fear, get it gear, and refocus on what mattered most in the last days with mom.

I made a conscious and intentional effort to **connect** and leverage what mattered most to me and why it mattered and remain laser focused on that. Next, I made sure my thoughts, words, and actions were laser focused and all **aligned** with my head and heart.

Additionally, I monitored my self-talk, my emotions, and my perspective constantly. If I discovered any of those three not supporting what mattered most to me, I worked on shifting any or all of them as quickly as I could to support my mission.

Finally, managing my emotions, tapping into, and engaging with mom and others utilizing emotional intelligence and emotional resilience strategies I'd been trained to use allowed me to stay in integrity with my commitment to be present for my mom, myself, and my family.

What I know now, that I didn't know then is that I was conditioning a four step process that allowed me to be present, congruent, and intentional with what mattered to me most for a little more than 21 days until it became an autopilot program I mastered unconsciously. It's the process I'm going to teach you to use to become a permanent non-smoker and create a smoke free habit.

Print out the next two pages and carry them with you as they will serve as your roadmap for developing a Smoke Free Habit using the 4 Step Smoke Free Process.

Create a Smoke Free Habit in 4 Steps

The key to creating a Smoke Free Habit is to CARE:

Step 1. Connect

Step 2. Align

Step 3. Refine

Step 4. Engage

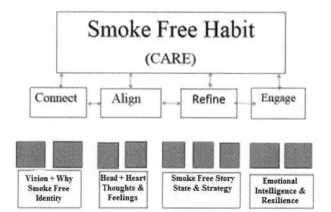

Habit Blueprint

Trigger   Routine   Reward

Trigger   Routine Anticipation Reward

Trigger   Routine   Craving   Reward

Trigger   Autopilot Response   Reward

**Smoke Free Habit Success = Change the Routine +
Create/Condition a New Habit**

Until =Autopilot Routine

Step 1: Connect

The gifts and lessons I received at mom's bedside and throughout her passing were many.

The experience offered a transformational opportunity for me to **connect** and gain clarity about the unconscious habits that were running my life and to make a conscious choice to reprogram the habits that weren't serving me, like smoking.

I discovered and uncovered a different perspective about the meaning of the power of choice, the meaning of life and death, and the power of your family tribe and how family habits, beliefs, rules, choices, emotional behaviors are subconsciously instilled throughout life and in the transition from life to death.

I had an opportunity to observe, experience and reflect on the power of the mind, body, spirit connection and how all three are impacted by the decisions your spirit makes.

I **connected** with and experienced, an unlimited number of times, the impact of the power of my emotions and discovered how my emotions (especially fear) triggered my survival switch and flooded my body with 40,000+ hormones in less than one heartbeat.

I walked out of the hospital three weeks later very clear that living life as I had known it both personally and professionally was no longer an option for me. I walked in with one set of beliefs, values, and perspective about life and walked out with a completely different set.

My new clarity and perspective about the connection and communication between the mind, body, and spirit opened up possibilities and provided me with the required freedom and courage to apply my new perspective and reinvent myself both personally and professionally.

I honored the commitment I'd made to mom and successfully stopped smoking. I used hypnosis and self-hypnosis to ensure my success. I connected with the fact that I walked in with one identity and set of beliefs, and walked out with another set. I walked in a smoking non-believer and walked out a non-smoking believer in hypnosis.

A believer in trying one more time even if you're completely convinced you'll fail again. A believer in turning off your autopilot switch, tapping in, tuning up, and allowing the wisdom of your heart intelligence to sync up and align with wisdom of your brain.

Most importantly, I walked out a believer in consciously choosing to live life authentically, vulnerably, and courageously instead of unconsciously distracting myself with cigarettes so I wouldn't or couldn't feel the fear I had of getting hurt if chose to live that way. And, I walked out a believer in loving and accepting myself unconditionally and demonstrated that by becoming a master at living a smoke free life.

What I didn't know then, that I am completely clear about now, after doing more than 6,000+ hypnosis sessions is this… most smokers have no idea when they began disconnecting from their emotions and allowing their auto pilot programming to kick in and turn on and hijack their dreams.

What they do understand but can't figure out how to change… is how to stop repeating the same emotional and behavioral patterns and start achieving an empowering result that makes them feel happy, fulfilled, and at peace.

I'm about to give you the secret sauce so you can stop trying, failing, and feeling bad about yourself and achieve the stop smoking success you want in 21 days.

Here's what I didn't know back then as a smoker that I know and want to share with you now is this:

Your smoking habit involves three distinct components including: a cue/trigger, a routine (smoking) and a reward. One would think that you have the ability to change anyone of the three and eliminate your smoking habit. That's just not the case.

In order to stop smoking permanently and create a Smoke Free Habit you MUST **CONNECT and DO THIS…replace/change your routine and condition the new routine until it become an unconscious automatic habit that your mind executes automatically.**

You'll NEVER be able to get rid of your triggers. You're hardwired to avoid pain and move toward pleasure or reward so that will never change. We are pleasure/reward seeking individuals. Your mind already knows how to create and does create automatic habits when you perform routine actions over and over.

Am I making sense now?

If you are committed and ready to get started right now:

Ask Your Self and Answer These Seven Important Questions:

1. Do you have a family member, friend, or peer group that you wanted to be like or be a part of that smoked?

_____

_____

2. What age were you the very first time you smoked?

_____

3. What emotion/s do you remember feeling right before you smoked your first cigarette?

_____

_____

4. What was the story you told yourself before and right after you smoked the first time to justify smoking?

_____

_____

5. What's the story you've been telling yourself recently to justify smoking?

_____

_____

_____

6: What are seven times throughout the day or evening when you smoke automatically without thinking?

_____

_____

_____

_____

7. What are five to seven activities you could to invest your time and enjoy doing instead smoking in the situations above?

_____

_____

_____

Strategy # 1:

Create a new smoke free identity, practice, and condition your new identity for 21 days BEFORE YOU STOP SMOKING.

What will you be thinking, saying, and doing as a non-smoker instead of what you're thinking, saying, and doing as a smoker? What will it feel like to be you as a non-smoker? How will you spend your time and money differently than you do now? What emotions will you experience? More confidence? More Self-esteem? What health benefits will you experience when you quit smoking?

Most of my clients are clear about the benefits they want to experience when they quit smoking but most haven't considered what living smoke free will be like or what they will be thinking saying or doing as a non-smoker.

That pre-planning makes the transition from living life as a smoker to living smoke free almost effortless. You'll have a blueprint to put into practice when life throws you lemons and you unconsciously reach for a smoke out of habit.

Strategy # 2:

Create Your Smoke Free Vision Board

Grab several of your favorite magazines and thumb through them carefully reading the headlines and looking at the pictures. Pay attention and notice how you feel, what you think, and the story you create in your mind about the picture or headline. Cut out those pictures and headlines that resonate with you.

Find/purchase a poster board and create your new identity and vision of a smoke free life. Begin placing the pictures and headlines that most clearly depict you living smoke free and modeling your smoke free identity.

The pictures should represent one or all of the thoughts, words, or actions that represent your new identity. Post that representation of you living a smoke free life someplace you'll see frequently.

Strategy # 3:

Click here to **Join the 21 Day Smoke Free Challenge** and grab your copy of the "50 Stop Smoking Hypnosis Suggestions" I'm giving away as a bonus when you join the challenge. When you join, I'll hold your virtual hand, whisper stop smoking hypnosis suggestions in your ear, and help you be ready to be smoke free forever in 21 days.

Then come back and finish reading the book.

Step 2: Align Your Head Heart Thoughts Words Actions

Have you ever made a conscious decision to think, say, or do one thing only to find yourself thinking, saying, or doing, something else? Your head and heart were not aligned. There are lots of reasons that might happen.

It happens all day long if you're not paying attention. If you've ever told yourself "I'm going to quit smoking" and later noticed yourself doing the opposite of that like picking up a smoke and lightening it, your head and heart were not aligned.

We make a conscious decision to think, say, or do one thing and the minute we shift our attention to something else our autopilot programming takes over. Here's why that happens:

Your conscious mind is responsible for completing all the logical, rational, and analytical things you need to do during the day. Your unconscious mind on the other hand is responsible for everything that happens automatically.

Think about how complicated life would become if you had to make a conscious decision to do all the automatic things your body does like, coughing, sneezing, laughing, breathing, moving, bending, etc... you get my point ☺ There's a good reason. We'd never get anything done otherwise.

The subconscious mind is essentially a huge data warehouse that stores all of you memories along with what you thought and felt about the experience you had.

Almost every stop smoking client I've worked with over the years walks in my door, sits down in the chair and declares 'You're my last resort I've tried everything else. I want to stop smoking and keep sabotaging myself.

It's like I have two different parts of my brain in a tug-of-war contest and I'm losing. I keep saying one thing and doing something else. "I'm ready to get my head, heart, thoughts, words and actions aligned and on the same page." Will hypnosis work? How long will it take?"

Ryan was one of those clients. Here's what I told him that you need to know.

Your unconscious mind is programmed to keep you alive and make sure you survive. It requires the assistance of the subconscious mind, the conscious mind, and rest of the body to make sure that happens. The subconscious mind his responsible for storing all your life experiences along with how you felt and what you thought when the experience happened. The conscious mind (willpower resides here) is the analytical rational part of the mind responsible for decision making. All three parts of your mind have played a role in your smoking habit and will continue to long after you stop smoking.

"You'll leave here in about two hours a non-smoker. Your job is to leave here today committed to condition, condition, condition, your new smoke free identity for the next 21 + days until it becomes your autopilot program and identity.

That's exactly what it takes to stop smoking today and remain smoke free forever." Just like me, he walked in a smoker, and walked out a non-smoking believer in the power of his subconscious mind, the power of hypnosis, and his ability to remain smoke free forever."

The key to quitting smoking, creating a smoke free habit, AND living smoke free forever is to consciously and consistently ensure your head, heart, thoughts, words, and actions are completely aligned on the same page.

Unless you are paying attention to how you are feeling physically and/or noticing what emotions you're feeling, your unconscious and subconscious mind will take over and begin running your autopilot programming (habits) and hijack your life. All you have to do if your discover you're out of sync is to refocus on your Smoke Free vision and why you want it, then realign your thoughts, words, and actions with your Smoke Free vision. When you do that enough it will become your autopilot Smoke Free Habit.

Ask Your Self and Answer These Seven Important Questions:

1. What are seven reasons why you've decided to quit smoking?

_____

_____

_____

_____

_____

2. What are seven benefits you want to receive or experience after quitting smoking?

_____

_____

_____

_____

3. What are seven statements you can tell yourself and others about choosing to be a permanent non-smoker?

_____

_____

_____

_____

4. What are three emotions you expect to experience or experience more of as a permanent non-smoker that you may not be experiencing as a smoker?

_____

_____

_____

_____

5. What are seven things you can do with the money you save when you quit smoking in 21 days?

_____

_____

_____

_____

6. What two to five people in your life will be the most excited about your decision to be smoke free?

_____

_____

_____

7. Who are the two to three individuals you would be willing to ask to serves as your support system the first 21 days you quit smoking?

_____

_____

_____

Strategy # 4- Create a Three Sentence Smoke Free Elevator Speech

Prepare a three sentence elevator speech to share with others when they invite you to smoke with them. Failure to do this will allow you to slip back into your old pattern once you stop.

Make sure your elevator speech is packed with plenty of words that express your conviction and commitment to do what it takes to be smoke free. Understand that your smoking friends will have a vested interest in getting you to come with them. Your decision, commitment, and conviction to stop forever forces them to look deep inside themselves and question if/why they haven't had the courage to do what you're doing.

Strategy # 5-Write 2 Letters to Your Smoke Free Self

Grab your journal and write two letters. Write the first letter to the younger non-smoking version of you and the second to an older non-smoking version of you 5 years from now.

Explain all the things you wish you had known then about smoking that you know now and what you would do differently if you had the opportunity to relive that moment in history again.

Use the exact language and emotion necessary to convince your younger you why you don't them to smoke. Be specific and graphic! Include any physical, mental, emotional, or spiritual concerns you're experiencing now that have developed as a result of your smoking.

Write a second letter to the older version of you and express your love, appreciation and gratitude for living smoke free for so long.

Strategy # 6- Create a one page Smoke Free Declaration of Independence

Include in your declaration the 7 + reasons why you've made a decision to stop smoking, 7+ activities you will commit to master while smoke free that will replace smoking and contribute to your mind, body, and spirit's health. Example: I plan to master walking 30 minutes 2X per day for the next 3 months.

Strategy # 7-Capture and Create a List of Your Old Disempowering Beliefs

Grab a sheet of paper or your journal. On the first piece of paper make a list of all the disempowering beliefs you've had and been telling yourself about quitting smoking. Two examples of disempowering beliefs I and a lot of my clients included: "I know if I quit smoking I'll gain weight" and "I'll stop smoking but start again the minute I gain 10 pounds."

What I know now, that I didn't know back then is I was sabotaging my stop smoking success and almost guaranteeing I wouldn't be successful. The thoughts and words you repeat again and again are essentially self-hypnosis suggestions and are filed away as a true belief in your subconscious mind. Your subconscious mind will access them as what's true for you in the future when you quit.

Strategy # 8-Capture and Create a List of Your New Empowering Beliefs

On the second piece of paper make a list of all the empowering beliefs you want to have or now have about quitting smoking. My favorite empowering belief I recommend you consider using is this: "I used to believe I'd gain 10 pounds if I quit smoking. I know now I can quit easily without gaining weight at all.

I know there's someone reading this right now thinking to themselves…

"I can say that all day long but I really don't believe it."

Am I right?

Here's what you need to know. Your mind is like a computer. Whatever you tell it, it will do. I doesn't know how to interpret fact from fantasy. Whether you tell it something empowering or disempowering over and over again it will store the information as fact. It's the old fake it until you make it strategy your mom told you about. She was right.

Strategy # 9- Grab Your Smoke Free Habit Communication Tool

Text #HabitTool to 1-512-640-2505 to receive a Smoke Free Habit Communication Tool you can use to reprogram your words to match your new Smoke Free identity. Let me hold your hand, whisper virtual words of wisdom on the page, and let's begin to explore who you are, who you're not, and who you will decide to be as your new non-smoking identity. Come right back here and finish reading the book.

Step 3-Refine Your Story, State, Strategy

It's that late night call that startles you awake and fills you with fear and dread. I picked up the phone and answered and a tiny voice on the other end whispered "Mom I've been in an accident and I'm hurt bad. Please get here quick, Mom I need you. How long will it take you to get here?

In less time than a heartbeat, my survival switch kicked on and my body was flooded with 40,000 hormones preparing me fight, flight, or freeze. I felt my body shift into a fight state as I promised my son I'd be there as fast as I could get there.

The urge to smoke both overwhelmed and surprised me as I hung up the phone. I hadn't smoked nor thought about smoking for many years. I made a conscious choice in the moment to tell myself the story "I Will Not Ever start smoking again," quickly shifted my focus elsewhere, and headed out of town to my son.

I traveled in the wee hours of the morning and made it to the hospital in 3 1/2 hours. My body and mind were traveling at a rate that felt like a thousand miles an hour while the speedometer on my dashboard registered only 95. In the theatre of my mind, my subconscious was performing a life review sorting though and examining both personal and professional crisis experience I'd experienced in   attempt to determine how to handle the crisis I was in. That little voice inside me was quietly whispering the story "Pull over and buy a pack no one will ever know."

One interesting thing I noted was that in every experience my subconscious mind examined I was either completely confident and in control managing the crisis or away from the crisis smoking. It helped me to understand why now as well as in the past fear triggered the urge to smoke.

Every memory it pulled out for review flooded my body with an additional 40,000 hormones. In those "Why Me Why Now Moments" thought provoking moments I remember telling myself "Gosh, I wish I had a cigarette. I know it would calm this feeling down."

Instead, I made a conscious choice to take deep breaths, shift my focus, reinvent my reality by imagining that I was sending powerful healing energy and love from my heart to my son's, and visualizing myself turning off my survival switch inside, turning my faith switch on, and handing my fears about my son over to God. In less than a heartbeat my body began to shift to a state of peace.

For those three and a half hours I remained committed to remain focused on managing my state, story, and strategy. I recognized I was at great risk for telling myself "Screw this! I Have to Have a Cigarette now" and doing exactly that.

Funny, but staying in complete alignment and making sure my story, state, and strategy were aligned with my vision and reasons to remain smoke free forever and turning the rest over for God to handle seemed to fire me up and keep me going.

My son survived the accident although his recovery and the rehabilitation required to heal his significant injuries took a while I feel blessed to say we both survived and discovered many miracles and gifts we gave ourselves and each other along the way.

One of the gifts I gave myself was to consciously choose to honor my commitment to remain smoke free forever and made sure my story, state, and strategy supported the vision. In the midst of crisis, I made a conscious choice over and over again to shift out of fear, remain focused and visualize my perfect result, believe and trust it would happen, and allow the power of love and faith to conquer the situation.

What I know now and knew back then if you choose to shift out of fear and shift into a state of love and appreciation miracles can and will happen. A very wise woman once told me "Whenever fear comes knocking send Faith to answer the door." It's a great story to tell yourself and strategy to use when you quit smoking, want to start again, or are afraid you'll never stop.

Ask Your Self and Answer These Seven Important Questions:

1. Think back to a time when you were the most afraid about a situation. How do you remember handling the situation?

_____

_____

_____

_____

2. Do you remember feeling 40,000 stress hormones flooding your body?

_____

_____

3. What did you do or what strategy did you use to get yourself back to a place of peace?

_____

_____

_____

_____

4. What self-talk did you tell yourself along the way?

_____

_____

_____

5. Do you notice a pattern in your self-talk?

_____

_____

_____

6. Is you self-talk mostly empowering or do you find
yourself frequently having a disempowering shame,
blame, shoulda conversation with yourself?

_____

_____

_____

7. What are three empowering statements you could use
in the future to support your WHY you've decided to be
smoke free forever? (Feel free to grab three from the 50
Self Hypnosis Suggestions if you're having a hard time)

_____

_____

_____

Practice aligning your story, state, and strategy with your vision.

Strategy # 10-Ask 5 Critical Questions & Gain Emotional Clarity Quickly

Anytime you notice that you're feeling an emotion you don't like. Ask yourself the following questions to get clarity about your immediate situation and discover if your survival switch turned on, made a decision you're in danger, and is preparing your body to fight, take flight, or flee.

The questions are designed to help you decide if you are really in danger or if your subconscious mind and unconscious mind are communicating a past or future experience in the moment and you need to step up and take charge.

Here are the questions: What am I feeling? Where is this feeling coming from? (Past, present, or future) What would I have to believe in order to feel this way? Is it true or just a story I'm telling myself because of something that happened in the past?

Strategy # 11-Turn Off Your Survival Switch

Close your eyes take a deep breath and lend me your imagination. Imagine that somewhere inside your body is a room we'll call your safe room. It's the place you go to get away anytime you need to be alone and feel safe to be yourself. Take a deep breath and go there now.

Walk in, close the door and lock it. Let everything and everybody outside this room take care of live without you and leave you alone for a little while.

Look around the room and notice that the room is a perfect place to go to rest. It has a beautiful couch that you can sit on and go ahead and do that now. Look around the room and notice that there appears to be a giant screen on one wall that looks like a movie screen.

On the other wall there appears to be a control panel along the wall almost like the control panel you see in the cockpit of an airplane. Walk over to the control panel, find the knob or switch labeled fear, and turn it all the way to the left right before it turns off. Now find the knob that's labeled relaxation and dial that knob all the way to the right as far as it will go right now. Imagine you place silver duct tape over both knobs to make them stay in place. Use this strategy anytime you're feel a feeling you don't like especially fear.

Strategy: 11- Turn On Your Relaxation Response

Close your eyes take a deep breath and take yourself back to your safe room in the theatre of your mind. Sit or lay down and get comfortable on the couch, the bed, or the chair. What I'd like for you to do now is lend me your imagination and pretend with your eyes closed that there's a ball of relaxing energy right above your head.

With your eyes still closed lookup through the top your head see a great big ball of relaxing energy vibrating gyrating right above your head. In just a minute count backwards silently to yourself from 3 down to 1.

As soon as you say the number three, allow yourself to feel and experience that warm relaxing energy drip down or roll down your body in a wave like motion from that ball of relaxing energy above your head.

Feel the warmth as it encompass and wraps in invisible protective layer around you. Notice how that almost feels the way you feel when you pull the covers back and slip into your warm cuddly bed at night.

Inside that invisible layer of protection around you notice that you finally feel safe Know that you can come here anytime and plug in and feel safe.

Use this strategy over and over again. Since your brain cannot tell the difference between reality and your imagination, the relaxation effects can be activated simply by using your imagination.   This is a great strategy to use to distract yourself from smoking urges or carvings.

Strategy 12: Grab Your 21 Day Smoke Free Conditioning Plan

Text #Plan to 1-512-640-2505 to receive your 21 Day Smoke Free Conditioning Plan. Then come back and finish the book.

Step 4: Engage and Allow Your Emotional Intelligence and Emotional Resilience to Flow As You Engage With Others

An emotion as a strong subjective feeling such as joy, sadness, fear. The critical word here is the word subjective because my definition of fear might not be the same definition as yours. That makes it subjective. So how one perceives and responds to an emotion they are feeling will always be dependent upon one's life experiences and the lens through which they view life.

Emotional Resilience is the emotional capacity or ability to prepare for, recover from, and adapt in the face of stress, challenge, or adversity.

Emotional Intelligence is the ability to detect and decipher your emotions, harness and use them appropriately based on the situation, understand and appreciate the slight variances among all emotions and how they evolve over time, and to regulate and manage our own emotions and those of others.

We learn how to be or not be emotionally intelligent and/or resilient long before we have the wisdom or choice to decide what either means much less if we are.

In our formative years (at least before age 6) our role models including family members, teachers, babysitters, all those people of influence that model their version of emotional intelligence for us, influence our version of what, how, and why emotions are, why they happen, and what to do with them.

As we experience our emotions, our subconscious is responsible for filing those experiences away in our memory bank and attaches how we felt and what we thought about the experience in the same file.

Those emotional experiences become our frame of reference for "what's normal" unless and until we decide that it's not. I often refer to it with clients as one's tribal emotions, tribal emotional intelligence and tribal emotional resilience.

What I've continued to be amazed by over the many years in practice especially after quitting smoking and becoming a hypnotherapist is how few of us have any basic education, training, or understanding of what our emotions are, where they come from, what we are supposed to do with them when we feel them, much less how to be emotionally intelligent or emotionally resilient when life defining "Why Me Why Now" moments happen over and over again.

Unless we are conscious in those moments, our tribal stuff gets activated and we respond automatically like someone in our tribe of origin did. Have you ever surprised yourself by saying or doing something the exact same way your mother or father did after swearing you'd never do that? Tribal conditioning was in play.

The important people in my life and family tribe smoked. Smoking became my emotional resilience default pattern. Until I became a committed non-smoker and boy was I surprised when I started telling myself the truth instead of the story I'd been telling myself for 37+ years.

I used smoking as my go to solution to prepare for, recover from, adapt in the face of every crisis, challenge, or adversity and avoid feeling what I didn't want to feel.

Every smoker I've ever worked with as a nurse, health coach, or hypnotherapist eventually comes to that realization. It's important for you to do that too. In order to live as a permanent non-smoker you'll have to make a conscious decision to use your emotions as your compass to determine when your survival switch turns on and consciously and consistently use empowering tools and strategies to prepare for, recover from, adapt in the face of crisis, challenge, or adversity instead of smoking.

Your mind know how to do it and does it automatically. All you have to do is wake up and consciously decide which strategies and tools to use.

Don't forget to remember. The story you've been telling yourself about quitting smoking and how hard it is or was to do is a lie you've been telling yourself forever. I should know, I told myself the same lie for 37 + years. It took me one two hour hypnosis session and 21 days of conscious, committed, conditioning of my new smoke free identity and several emotional resilience strategies to finally free myself.

I'm committed to make sure you're successful this time and you live smoke free forever.

Ask Your Self and Answer These Seven Important Questions:

1. How many times this week did you find yourself struggling with your emotions?

_____

_____

_____

2. What was the most common emotional state you felt?

_____

_____

_____

3. How long did the struggle in that emotional state last? How often do you feel this emotion?

_____

_____

_____

4. Do you know what triggered the emotion you were feeling?

_____

_____

_____

5. Was smoking a tool you used to pull out of your emotional state?

_____

_____

_____

6. Do you feel smoking shifted you to a more empowering emotional state?

_____

_____

_____

7. What other tools did you use to change your emotional state?

_____

_____

_____

Strategy # 13- Emotional Resilience Instant Replay

Grab a piece of paper or your journal and make a list of the Top 10 Most Memorable Moments of your life. Include those events and times you felt powerful, relaxed, happy, accomplished, peaceful, confident, certain, compassionate, loving, calm. It's important for you to include a variety of experiences.

As you create your list spend some time recalling all the details of the experience. Details like who you were with, what you were doing, where you were, how it felt, which of your senses were activated smell, taste, touch. Notice how your body feels as you take a trip down memory lane.

Carry your list with you and when you feel the urge or desire to smoke, take a time out from smoking, and practice the visualization strategy below instead of smoking. Notice how relaxed you feel after doing this visualization for 5-10 minutes.

Strategy # 14-Practice & Perform an Emotional Resilience Release

Anytime you feel an emotion you don't like to feel and need to get back to a state of balance here's what you can do.

Close your eyes, take five deep breaths, and take yourself to your safe room in the theatre of you mind.

Walk in, close the door, and lock it. Sit in a chair, relax, and take yourself back to one of your Top Ten Memorable Moments. See yourself on your movie screen in your safe room. Allow yourself to re-experience that Magic Moment again. Imagine you can taste, smell, feel, hear, and see everything again the same way it happened the very first time you experienced it. Turn the volume up on your senses.

Pay attention to the way your body feels. Notice the shift in your emotions and your physical body. Allow yourself to feel those magical feelings over and over. Here's why it is important to turn the volume up on your senses. You brain is unable to distinguish between reality and imagination.

However, when you make a conscious effort to re-experience these important positive experiences, your body releases important hormones that release your endorphins and allow your body to reset itself to an empowering state of balance and relaxation.

You can use this strategy anytime anywhere. Anytime you're feeling disempowered, anytime you hear yourself telling a disempowering story, take yourself to that safe place in your mind and shift yourself to a different state, place, and time.

It will become an important part of your emotional resilience tool chest when you stop smoking.

Strategy # 15-Practice & Perform an Emotional State Review

Grab a piece of paper or your journal. Make a list of five-seven disempowering emotions/emotional states you experience on a regular basis. Rank the emotions on your list according to the frequency in which you experience them. For example rank #1 as the emotion you experience most often and # 7 as the one that happens occasionally.

In addition, list two to three people, events, or situations that trigger each of the emotions. Place a star beside the emotions that cause you to reach for a smoke. Notice if you see a pattern in the relationship between your smoking and a particular emotion.

Strategy # 16-Practice & Perform an Emotional State Redo

Grab a piece of paper or your journal. Make a list of five-seven empowering emotions/emotional states you WANT to experience on a regular basis. Rank the emotions on your list according to the frequency in which you want to experience them.

Now, fully describe what you would be thinking, saying, doing, feeling as well as how your body would appear in each of those five-seven empowering emotional states.

Make a conscious effort to practice living in each of your desired states for at least 15 minutes a day for the next 21 days. Keep a journal of your experiences while practicing.

When you feel an urge or desire to smoke take a time out, choose an empowering emotional state, and make a conscious decision to practice being in that state for at least fifteen minutes before giving yourself permission to smoke.

Strategy # 17-Grab Your Copy of 21 + Emotional Resilience Power States Blueprint

Text #PowerStates to 1-512-640-2505 to receive your copy of the Emotional Resilience Power States Blueprint. Then come right back and finish the book.

Condition, Condition, Condition.

If you are like me and you've tried everything possible to stop smoking without success, you almost certainly have a try, fail, and feel bad about yourself pattern running in the background of your life sabotaging your stop smoking success.

If I knew then what I now, it would have only taken one time to become smoke free forever. However, you don't know what you don't know until you know it.

Pay attention to this chapter. I've included the secret sauce to be smoke free forever here.

What I didn't know then that I know now is that you absolutely, positively, MUST HAVE:

A. A vision of your new smoke free identity

B. A Smoke Free Blueprint for Success

C. A 21 day Conditioning Plan

Quitting smoking is EASY is easy to master. I was a Master at quitting smoking. Living Smoke Free was just as easy to master but I made it hard and didn't know it until knew and understood how to master it.

Make sure you have A-C above and Repeat steps 1-3 below to condition your new non-smoking identity until it becomes your autopilot program. Remember it takes 21 days to create a new habit and about four months to develop unconscious competence or in other words your autopilot program.   .

1. **See It**- See yourself as a non-smoker (**Go to the Theatre of the Mind**)

2. **Believe It**- Believe it's possible you're a non-smoker (**Tell Yourself You Are Smoke Free Forever**)

3. **Be It**- Act like you're a non-smoker (**Don't put anything in your mouth and light it**)

Condition, Condition,

Steps 1-3 for 21 days. DO NOT PUT A CIGARETTE OR ANYTHING ELSE IN YOUR MOUTH AND LIGHT IT.

The reason I failed so many times is because when I felt an emotion or a feeling I didn't like I failed to make a consciously committed effort to execute 1-3 AND

I conditioned myself over and over and over again with stupid stuff like:

1. This is soooooooooo hard.

2. I can't do this!

3. I hate the way I feel!

4. We all die of something I'll just keep smoking!

5. I need a cigarette.

6. I've got to have a cigarette.

7. I'm so irritable I could kill someone.

8. I'm so hungry I could eat a horse.

9. Damn, I need a cigarette.

10. I'm a failure again. I'm going to the store to buy a pack. Just call me a loser.

Don't do what I did. Use the strategies below to condition, condition, condition, your new identity, create a new chapter in your Stop Smoking Story, create your Smoke Free Habit as you prepare for you Stop Smoking Date with Destiny.

Strategy 18-Practice a Smoke Free Visualization & Release

Close your eyes, take a deep breath, and imagine that you're driving into the parking lot of your favorite movie theater. Park, get out of your car, walk up to the front and buy a ticket. Grab the ticket, walk in and move forward toward the refreshment center. Buy yourself some popcorn and something to drink. While waiting, look both directions and find the theatre with a marquee that has your name on the marquee.

Walk toward the room with your name on the marquee. Open the door, walk in, and stand by the door a minute and let your eyes accommodate the darkness you are standing in. Notice that as your eyes adjust you begin to move forward.

Visualize yourself moving forward, intentionally walking up the stairs or down the stairs and finding the perfect place to sit. You are the only one in the theater so this time you get to sit wherever you want to. Sit down and find the remote control underneath your chair.

Now count quietly in your mind, from three down to one and when you say the number one, notice two things. Sitting right beside you is a younger version of you.

The younger version of you is the exact age you were the moment before you started smoking. Notice that the two of you have shifted your fearful "I'm Not Enough" energy. Both you and younger you are now on the screen in front of yo9u, smiling with a twinkle in your eyes.

Quick, hit the pause button on your remote. Your job today is to convince that younger version of you to stop smoking. We're going to give to younger you a gift.

It's called a life re-do. Our job is to make sure she knows exactly what she needs to know so she can move through life as you, and experience every experience you've had to date, without ANY NEGATIVE CONSEQUENCES, and with all the resources she'll need so she never has to smoke to feel better about herself.

Take a deep breath, make a mental note of every single reason you've decided to quit smoking. Be sure to include everything you wish you'd known back then about smoking that is true for you right now.

Now, put your arms around that little person, turn around, look at him/her and in your most convincing voice and tell that younger version of you all the reasons he/she absolutely positively CANNOT EVER CHOOSE to smoke. Convince younger you now and take as long as you need.

When you're convinced with absolute certainty, you said everything you could or needed to convenience your little peep to make the commitment to never ever smoke, give him/her a hug and focus back on the screen in front of you.

Watch as the scene unfolds and your younger you makes a decision not to smoke. Watch him/her walk away from that almost started smoking experience as a non-smoker and remains smoke free for life.

Rewind that scene ten times and watch it over, and over, and over again.

Now, this last time, watch younger you turn, walk away, and listen and she says "No, thanks I'm not a smoker and never will be. Watch that younger version of you on the screen get smaller and smaller and smaller and smaller and smaller.

Now see a really younger version of you (less six years old) sitting on your lap. Imagine you're having a conversation with 6 year old you and the older "I'm Not a Smoker and Never Will Be" version of you while less than six sits in your lap. The three of you, in a dome shape room, sitting beside each other quietly talking.

Next, make a commitment and a declaration that you're going to stop smoking and remain smoke free forever. Be sure and name a date. Tell them both WHY you've decide to stop smoking and live smoke free forever.

From this moment forward, every time you get the urge or desire to smoke, imagine yourself putting a cigarette and lighting in the mouth of those two little earlier versions of you. Visualize that scene over and over again. Notice how it makes you feel when they start coughing and gasping for air.

If it's possible find an actual picture of those two earlier versions of you. Carry those pictures around with you and every time you feel the urge or desire to smoke pull those images out, remember your commitment to them, and repeat this exercise.

Remaining smoke-free is a choice and it requires that you make the choice to be a non-smoker every time you feel the urge or until it becomes an unconscious habit and part of your identity.

Good news is that it only takes 21 days to create a new habit and about four months to develop your permanent identity and unconscious competence living smoke free as a non-smoker.

Strategy 19-Perform a Smoke Free Belief Release

Grab the list of Disempowering Beliefs you documented in Strategy # 7. Grab your lighter and your list and take them outside to your barbecue pit or another place that's safe and appropriate for you to burn your list. Take a deep breath and set fire to those old disempowering beliefs that are no longer a part of your beliefs or story.

They were lies you've been telling yourself about who you are and why you smoke. Make a conscious effort to watch as you release the hold those beliefs had on you and your ability to free yourself from smoking.

Take a deep breath and breathe in the confidence, commitment, certainty, consciousness, creativity, and curiosity. Those are just a few of the emotional states you'll take with you on your smoke free journey moving forward as a non-smoker. Congratulations you've released your disempowering stories and beliefs and almost ready to be smoke free forever.

Strategy 20- Select a Smoke Free Success Song & Self-Hypnosis Suggestion

First, pick a song you love to listen to, makes you smile inside, and feel good about your life. If it resonates with you, makes you smile inside, and gives you energy, download it and use it as the ringtone on your phone for 21 Days.

Here's why, songs are great way to neutralize old programming, reset your state, and rediscover powerful parts of yourself.

Next, select several Self- Hypnosis Suggestions from the 50 Self-Hypnosis Suggestions PDF you received when you joined the 21 Day Challenge.

Each time you phone rings and your ringtone begins to play make a conscious and consistent effort to declare the self-hypnosis suggestion out loud if possible or silently to yourself. The self-hypnosis suggestion will help neutralize and replace any disempowering beliefs you have about successfully becoming smoke free!

Strategy 21-Select Your Smoke Free Support Team

Ask two individuals, a friend, a family member, or a spouse to be your accountability partner and support you on your Smoke Free journey for 21 days. Their job is to remind you of your strengths and ability to complete the journey if you have trouble along the way.

Now You Are Ready to……

See It. Believe It. Be It. Smoke Free Forever.

Complete the 21 Day Stop Smoking Challenge prior to you Smoke Free Stop Day.

On Day 22 listen to the 30 minute Stop Smoking Hypnosis Session (link below) and the Stop Smoking Forever!

Listen to the Smoking Hypnosis Session as often as you need to help Condition Your New Identity until it Becomes Automatic.

The Stop Smoking Hypnosis session is my gift to you for having the courage to trust me, try one final time, stop smoking, and live Smoke Free Forever!

All you need to do to get your Stop Smoking Hypnosis session is to send a copy of your receipt for this book to join-quitsmoking@instantcustomer.com and the link to the hypnosis session will be sent immediately.

Hypnosis VS Self-Hypnosis

Hypnosis was the tool that helped me finally quit smoking permanently after 37+ years. What was different for me the last time I quit was that living smoke free became my new identity.

I believe it worked because I finally understood that I could use the power of my subconscious and unconscious mind to do what they do automatically 24/7 and give myself permission to stop struggling to quit smoking and let it happen automatically. It really was that easy.

What I didn't know back then that I'm absolutely convinced of now is that all of us float in and out of a hypnotic trance all day long and have no idea we are doing it.

When you FOCUS and concentrate on something at work or at home you are actually in a hypnotic trance because the definition of hypnosis is simply a focused state of concentration. When you focus and apply all your concentration to one thing and block everything else out, you are by definition doing self-hypnosis.

Here's why that's so important for you to know.

What you are thinking, saying, processing, hearing, watching, and feeling while in a state of focused concentration is being filed and stored away in your subconscious mind permanently.

Your subconscious and unconscious mind will use that information again to process and determine what to say, think, or do if/when you are in a similar situation again at a later date.

All the stuff you've told yourself and others along you smoking journey is stored in your smoking file and is literally keeping you stuck in the habit of smoking.

I was totally freaked out when I realized I was responsible for keeping me in my stop smoking prison because of all the stuff I'd been thinking, saying, and doing all those years of smoking.

Just for starters, "I can't quit," "If I gain 5 pounds I'll start smoking again because I refuse to get fat," "I'm a failure because I can't quit" were just a few of the self-hypnosis suggestions I declared over and over again throughout the years.

I just didn't know then what I know now. You don't know something you don't know until you know it.

So, I'm sharing this information so you will know and understand that you my dear friend are doing self-hypnosis all day long and either ensuring or sabotaging your success.

If you make a conscious and consistent effort for 21 days to fill your subconscious mind with thoughts, words, and beliefs that support you to live smoke free and let your mind do what it does automatically, you too can live smoke free!

Just a few more facts about hypnosis and how to use self-hypnosis to create and support your smoke free habit.

Hypnosis is a state of focused concentration or consciousness. Self-Hypnosis is too. Hypnosis enhances your ability to use your subconscious mind or imagination to remember, use your creative abilities, and to respond to suggestions for change.

Your or a hypnotherapist guides you into a state of hypnosis by giving you simple instructions. It is like playing Simon Says. While you are focused on the instructions your conscious mind naturally closes down allowing your subconscious mind to open.

A hypnotherapist is a guide or a coach who employs hypnosis not only to give you suggestions for change, but to help you discover your true reasons for resisting change, and then enabling you to release those causes.

When the root cause of a problem or any mental blocks are released, your mind is free to respond to and accept positive suggestions for change. A hypnotherapist also helps you discover how to experience well-being by motivating you to use your own inner resources in ways that promote health and wellness.

Your thoughts or statements can either be empowering, neutral, or disempowering you and sabotaging your success. The interpretation or meaning you give your thoughts or words gives it an emotional charge.

All your thoughts and words are filed away in your history file by your subconscious and later used to interpret the meaning of something that is happening in the moment.

It's really important thing for you to know that when you repeat something over and over again either out loud or inside your head you are essentially doing self-hypnosis, your subconscious is storing the information as your truth, and whatever you're thinking or saying to yourself eventually becomes a belief AND a self-fulfilling prophecy.

I'm passionately committed to your success and hope that I have an opportunity to meet you in person sometime in the near future so I can give you a hug and hear your share your stop smoking success story and proudly declare loudly…..

#BecauseofYourBook "I Stopped Smoking and I'm Living Smoke Free Forever!"

I'd love to hear your success story and Celebrate Your Success! Send an email to support@SmokeFreeHabit.com with #BecauseofYourBook "I Stopped Smoking and I'm Living Smoke Free Forever!" or join my Facebook page and I'll enter your name into my monthly give away contest.

XOXO

Nancy Philpott, R.N.

Printed in Great Britain
by Amazon

29832145R00035